Write All About It

Activities for the Writing Process
Grades 1, 2, 3

Written by: John and Patty Carratello

The authors wish to thank Syndi Hillis for her valuable help.

Illustrated by: Keith Vasconcelles

Children greet life daily with zest. They observe, play, create, wonder, feel, and dream. As teachers, we can guide them in writing about their experiences in a creative and exciting way. This 80 page reproducible book will show you how to help your students enjoy and understand the writing process. First in a series of four books, this book provides an introduction to the writing process and related activities that will teach, reinforce, and strengthen writing skills. Pre-writing techniques, audience-awareness activities, revision strategies, post-writing suggestions, and cross-curricular connections are just a few of the ideas included to support the teaching of writing.

We know that with the ideas presented in this book both you and your students will look forward to writing each day.

Table of Contents

Teacher Created Materials, Inc.
P.O. Box 1040
Huntington Beach, CA 92647
©1993 Teacher Created Materials, Inc.
Made in U.S.A.

ISBN 1-55734-500-7

Tips for the Writing Program

◆ Create an atmosphere for writing. Fill the room with the written word in books, magazines, comic strips, cereal boxes, t-shirts, student writing, teacher writing, newspaper articles, record album notes, and any other appropriate stimulating writing.

◆ Include a daily writing period in your schedule.

◆ Keep all work in a writing folder. Students can keep their personal lists of words, topics, and ideas in their individual folders.

◆ Design a writing center, complete with a review of the writing process, sample activities for each stage in the process, a tub for writing folders, and writing materials. Use the patterns and labels on pages 4 and 5 to help decorate your center.

2

Tips for the Writing Program *(cont.)*

◆ Designate a spot for conferencing, and conference with a small group of students during writing time. Focus on one student's work at a time, allowing the student to "run" the conference by talking through his or her own work. Help guide each author with comments and questions, and encourage others in the writing group to offer suggestions and comments as well.

◆ Encourage students to write in small groups and discuss their writing in these groups. These "writing circles" often give students a safe, friendly place to create and revise. Writing time does not have to be silent time!

◆ Ask students to keep personal lists of words, quotes, and ideas that can be used to generate writing in the future. Any items that spark curiosity and enthusiasm should be included.

◆ Write in journals regularly. You may choose to begin the day with a teacher or student-generated journal topic, and allow time for freewriting. You can write too, or use the time for classroom management responsibilities.

◆ Model and participate in all writing activities yourself. Let your students know that you value writing, and can use the writing process successfully, too!

◆ Encourage illustration. Many students "turn on" to writing when they illustrate their own words.

◆ Share the writing generated in your class or by your students when they are outside your class. Students need to write for an audience other than the teacher. They also enjoy hearing what others have to say!

◆ Make a "Writers' Showcase" bulletin board. Give it a prominent place in the classroom. "Publish" the best work of your students there.

◆ Extend your students' writing to audiences beyond your class. Swap papers with classes at the same or different schools. Share finished work with parents. Invite the principal to select writing samples for display. Submit student writing to local publications. Publish a school magazine. Enter local, state, or national contests. Expand the audience for your students!

Center Signs

Display the following sign at your classroom writing center.

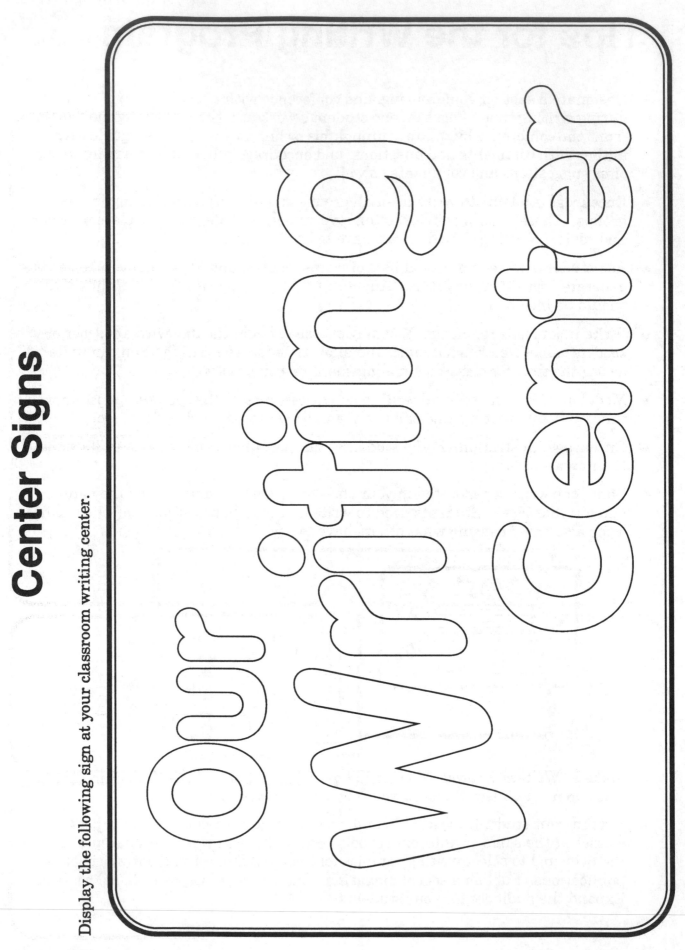

4

Center Signs *(cont.)*

Use the following signs to help you organize your writing center.

Pre-Writing

First Draft Writing

Response

Post Writing

Make Your Own Books

Revision

Editing and Rewriting

Evaluation

Writing Folders

Supplies

The Writing Process

The Writing Process presents the steps of writing in a methodical, sequential way, that is easily learned and assimilated by writers of all ages.

Pre-writing

First Draft Writing

Response

Revision

Editing and Rewriting

Evaluating

Post-writing

Although the steps of this process appear in linear arrangement above, they do not need to remain so as writers create. All stages, such as the pre-writing or response stages, can be revisited at any time in the process.

A "Writing Process Wheel" communicates the idea that the writing process is not linear, but open-ended. Directions and materials for the construction of this wheel are given below and on page 7.

Directions:

1. Cut out the "Writing Process Wheel" and arrow from page 7.

2. Color each section of the wheel a different color.

3. Laminate the wheel and arrow for longer use.

4. Attach the arrow to the center point of the wheel with a brad.

5. Display the finished wheel in your writing center, adjusting the arrow to the area of the writing process you have as a focus.

6. Encourage students to make their own wheels. With "personalized" wheels, it may be easier for them to remember and use the steps of the writing process!

Writing Process Wheel

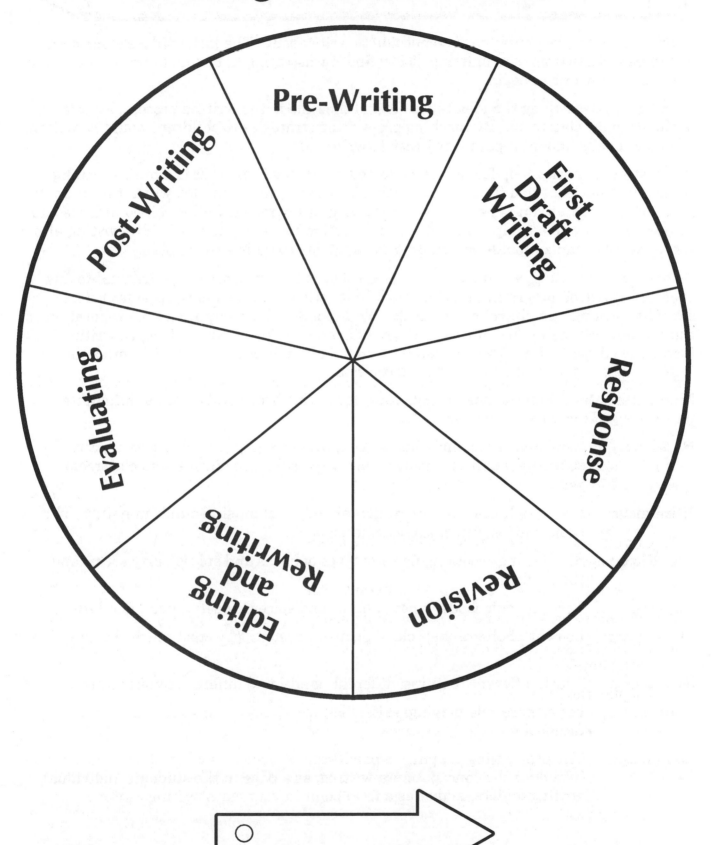

Pre-Writing Activities

In order to write, you must have something to write about. The lack of ideas stops many would-be writers from ever starting. They find it frustrating to be told to write when they have no idea where to begin.

Getting and developing the idea takes most of the time in the writing process, especially in the primary classroom. By teaching pre-writing strategies to children, would-be writers can more easily and less "painfully" start to write.

Pre-writing activities help formulate ideas before writing begins. It is a brainstorming stage, one that leads to a fluency of thoughts that can produce an idea which the students may want to capture on paper. This step in the writing process builds self-confidence and self-esteem, as well as helps to create the motivation necessary to write. Pre-writing also serves as an organizational tool, guiding the students in their writing plan.

As teachers of writing, we must keep in mind that pre-writing activities are vital to any successful writing program. A writer must first activate the thought processes before actually forming any kind of a first draft. While some writers require more preparation than others, all writers benefit by this type of beginning idea search. The pre-writing techniques described in this book can be used to build process writing skills, or as the initial stage or stages of specific writing projects.

Many ideas other than the suggestions provided in this book can be used to stimulate pre-writing. Here are just a few.

Reading: Read literature, including stories, poems, and plays; newspapers; cereal boxes; magazines; t-shirts; maps; logs; journals; diaries; and classroom walls!

Listening: Listen to literature; instrumental and vocal music; sounds in nature; TV; radio; videos; films; and commercials.

Smelling: Smell things cooking; flowers; types of herbs and spices; dirty socks; and the outdoors.

Tasting: Taste specific foods; types of herbs and spices; sweets, sours, and bitters.

Observing: Look at photographs; colors; pictures; posters; objects; nature; doodles; and each other.

Touching: Touch different textures; different hands; and different temperatures.

Doing: Experience role playing; skits; field trips; classroom guests; and creative dramatics.

Graphic: The pre-writing graphic on page 9 can be used as a coloring project to introduce the concept of pre-writing, as a page in the students' individual writing folders, and/or as a focal point in your class writing center.

Pre-Writing

Pre-Writing Ideas

Brainstorming

In brainstorming, students supply all the ideas they have on a specific topic. No judgments are made, as long as the ideas they contribute are appropriate to mention in class.

Brainstorming activities can be done individually, with a partner, in a small group, or as a class. Many students enjoy brainstorming in a small group, then sharing their group's ideas with the entire class.

Example

Brainstorming topic: What I can do on a rainy day . . .

- sleep
- bake cookies
- read to myself
- read to someone else
- play indoor basketball
- play checkers
- build a model
- make doll clothes
- play an instrument
- build with blocks
- walk in the rain
- watch television
- measure rainfall
- play cards
- paint
- work on the computer
- make puppets
- write letters
- wash dishes
- draw
- make a scrapbook
- write stories
- clean my room
- play with pets
- sing songs
- listen to the rain

Have your students use the half page form on page 11 for brainstorming other topics.

Free-Write

In free-writing, students write for a specified amount of time on a self-selected or teacher-selected topic. The focus of free-writing is not mechanics, but the fluency of ideas. Journals provide excellent places for free-writing experiences.

Ask your students to free-write on one or more of the topics below for five minutes. Encourage them to support their ideas with reasons.

- A pet I have or would like to have . . .
- What makes me laugh . . .
- How I feel about summer (or fall, winter, or spring) . . .
- The job I would like to have when I'm older . . .
- What I like doing most after school . . .

Your students may use the form on page 11.
Ask them to write the focus of their free-write as the title of their paper.

Brainstorming Ideas:

_____
Topic

If you have any more ideas, list them on the back of this page.

Free-Write

_____
Topic

Use the back of this page if you need more room for your free-write.

Clustering

In clustering, students diagram supporting ideas around a main idea. The cluster can accommodate all brainstormed ideas. This technique is particularly useful for visually-oriented learners.

Here is an example of clustering around the main idea of favorite smells.

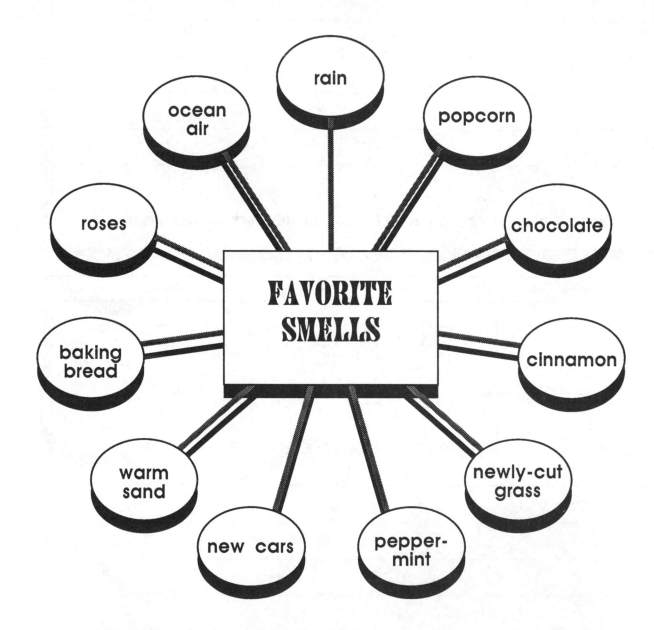

Ask your students to cluster their ideas for these or other topics on the clustering form provided on page 13. Clustering bubbles may be added as needed.

• pets	• sports	• holidays	• favorite books	• fears
• cars	• hobbies	• popular toys	• glass things	• "B" names

Clustering

Write your main idea in the center rectangle. Then write all your supporting ideas in the open bubbles. Add more bubbles if necessary.

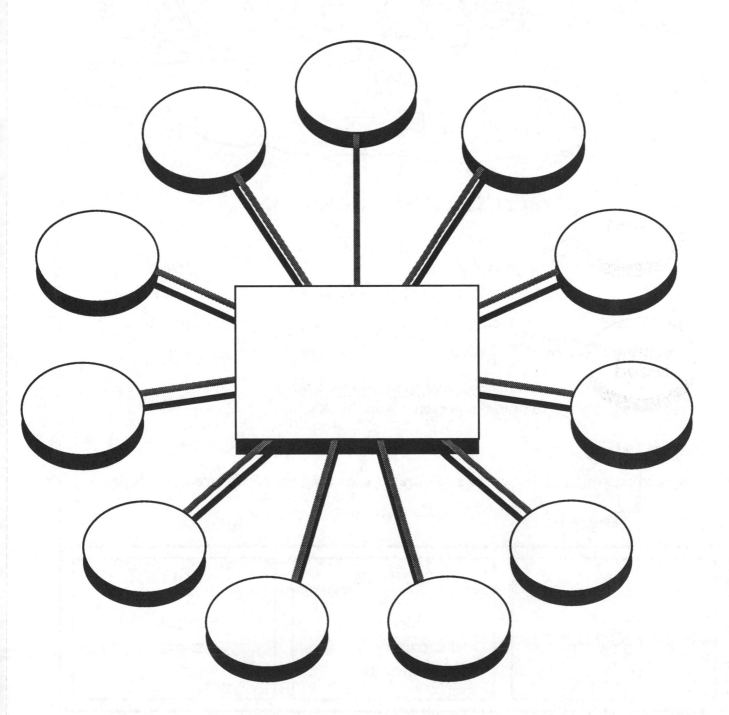

Word or Idea Banks

In a word or idea bank, students brainstorm all the words or ideas that pertain to a specific topic. The words and ideas can be "banked" on a wall chart or sheet of paper for high visibilty and ease of use.

"SUMMER FUN" WORD BANK

swimming	sleeping	baseball	tents
eating	reading	horseback	squirt guns
watermelon	riding	camping	picnics
popsicles	vacation	beaches	sun

Have students use page 15 to make personal word banks.

Categorizing

In categorizing, students list words and phrases according to specific areas of a topic.

Example

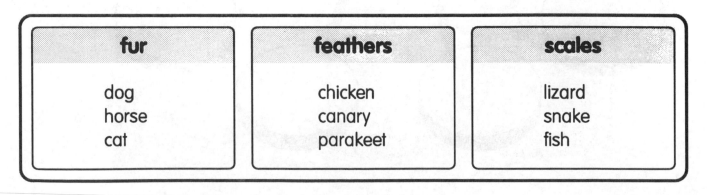

fur	feathers	scales
dog	chicken	lizard
horse	canary	snake
cat	parakeet	fish

Have students use page 16 to practice categorizing.

Word and Idea Banks

Collect all the words or ideas you can on a specific subject and ''deposit'' them in the ''bank'' below.

Topic: _____

Categories

Complete each box below.

Topic: Sports	
ball sports	**non-ball sports**

Topic: October			
food	**colors**	**activities**	**weather**

16

Venn Diagrams

When using a Venn diagram, students compare and contrast people, animals, places, or things. Similar qualities are written in the space two circles have in common, and dissimilar qualities are written in the areas the circles do not share.

Here is an example of the comparing and contrasting of two friends.

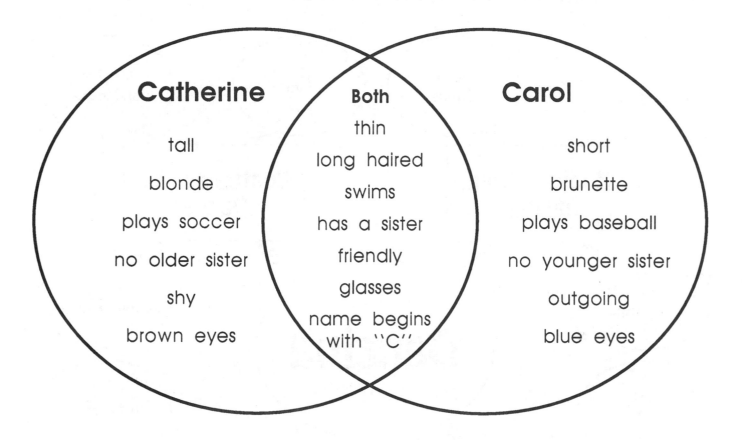

Catherine

tall

blonde

plays soccer

no older sister

shy

brown eyes

Both

thin

long haired

swims

has a sister

friendly

glasses

name begins with "C"

Carol

short

brunette

plays baseball

no younger sister

outgoing

blue eyes

Challenge your students to make Venn diagrams comparing and contrasting their best friends and themselves. After they understand how to pre-write by using a Venn diagram, encourage them to use this technique when comparing and contrasting other things. Here are some ideas.

- characters in stories
- specific animals
- specific plants
- types of sports
- you and a friend
- books

- seasons
- types of food
- careers
- siblings
- colors
- movies

- hobbies
- subjects in school
- vehicles
- pets in your home
- world leaders
- television shows

Mind Mapping

In mind mapping, students write a topic in the center circle and fill the remaining circles with ideas that clearly support the topic. It is similar to clustering, in that ideas are clustered around a main topic. However, mind maps show more organizational development, and can be extended to include areas that add detail to some or all of the supporting areas.

For example, a mind map for Dancing might look like this.

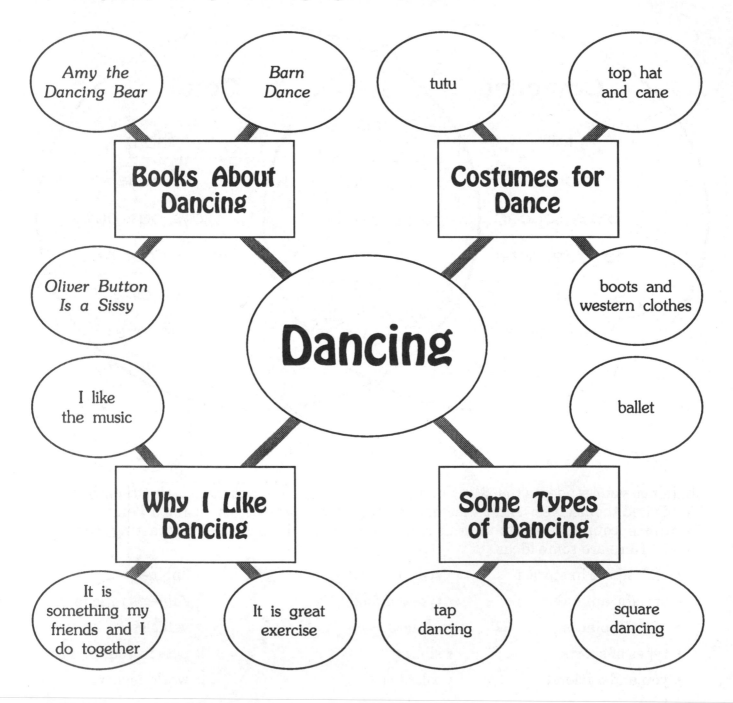

Have your students use page 19 to practice mind mapping.

Mind Mapping

Write your main topic in the center oval. Then choose three or four ideas that clearly support your main focus. Write them in the boxes. Develop each of these supporting ideas in at least three different ways in the small ovals.

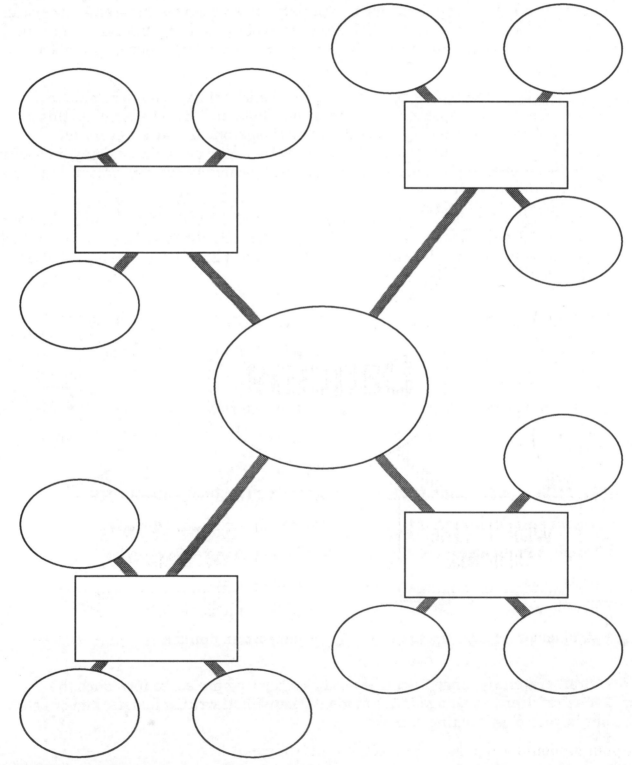

First Draft Writing Activities

Most of what a student writes should be first draft writing. First draft writing is always just a rough draft. As a teacher, especially as one who teaches beginning writers, you should stress that the purpose of first draft writing is to get ideas down in a semi-logical manner, not to spell, punctuate, or use form correctly. Students should have many more copies of first drafts in their writing folders than final drafts. In this way, they will have a "treasure chest" full of writing from which to pull ideas! As the year progresses, they can select a favorite first draft to take through more steps of the writing process. Continually remind your students that first draft writing is not finished writing, but a springboard to reach a final draft.

Students, especially those experiencing writing for the first time, need to be able to express their thoughts on paper without fear of the "Red Pen." Teachers can do this in many different ways. One way is to have students choose one first draft every ten assignments that they will take to final draft. The other nine assignments may have been shared with the teacher, a partner, the class, a parent, or just kept in the folder, but have not been graded in the traditional way.

Once students have collected pre-writing ideas, they need a purpose for writing. Without direction, first draft writing can wander aimlessly, especially when children have not had previous writing experience. Here are a few styles of writing, and samples of activities that can guide the assignments.

SENSORY/DESCRIPTIVE

(to describe in vivid detail)

- journal entries
- advertising copy
- character sketches
- poems

PRACTICAL/INFORMATIVE

(to present basic information)

- telephone messages
- post cards
- news reports
- summaries

IMAGINATIVE/NARRATIVE

(to tell what happens, to sequence)

- captions
- short stories
- fairy tales
- story boards

ANALYTICAL/EXPOSITORY

(to explain, analyze, persuade)

- letters to the editor
- commercials
- book or music reviews
- support an opinion

The first draft graphic on page 21 can be used as a coloring project to introduce the concept of a first draft, as a page in the students' individual writing folders, and/or as a focal point in your class writing center.

First Draft

Which of my first drafts is my favorite?

Types of Writing

Descriptive

Sometimes it is easier for students to start writing when they have a model. For example, asking students to describe their experience with snow might be easier if they read the excerpt about snow from Margaret Wise Brown's *The Important Book*.

Using Margaret Wise Brown's frame and their own clustering of ideas on a topic, students can easily create their own descriptive, sensory poems using the form at the top of page 23.

Imaginative

There are many ways to promote writing through the use of pictures. Using intriguing pictures from magazines, newspapers, books, or other sources, teachers can ask questions such as these to encourage written response: "What happened just before this picture was taken or drawn?" "What happens next in this picture?" "Use your imagination to explain what is going on in the picture." "Who is the person in the picture? Make up a name, and write a character profile about him or her, including such things as hobbies, likes, dislikes, and a personal background." "Is this picture the beginning, middle, or end of a story? Tell it!"

You may also wish to combine several pictures and ask the children to make up a story in which the characters from the different pictures meet.

At the bottom of page 23 there is a picture prompt to help your students get started. You can attach the picture to the center of a bulletin board and encircle it with the student writing it has generated.

Practical

Students need to realize that writing is a part of everyday life. Composing want ads is one practical form of writing that almost everyone experiences during their lives. To begin this activity with your students, study ads that *you and they* have been collecting from the paper. Point out qualities that the ads have in common and how they differ from "regular" writing. Then, as a class, practice writing ads by making one up to sell something from the classroom. Page 24 can then be used for individual writing.

Persuasive

In all writing, students need an idea of the "audience" who will read the piece of writing. Teachers of writing must sometimes direct students to different audiences in order to give a more direct purpose for specific writing assignments. When writing to persuade, writers must keep in mind who they are trying to convince, and present logical, reasonable arguments. Use page 25 to help your students practice persuasive writing.

Expository

Expository writing gives information or explains something. It is one of the most common forms of writing. Most school reports and "How To" manuals are done in this form. An expository paragraph usually begins with a sentence which states the main idea and is followed by sentences containing many supporting details. Practice this writing form by giving your students topic sentences and letting them research and write the details. For example: "Elephants are amazing mammals." "There are volcanoes on almost every continent." "It is easy to make a peanut butter sandwich."

The important thing about _____ is

that _____

_____

_____

_____

and _____

But the most important thing about _____ is

that _____

Want Ad

Your parents have given you permission to sell something from your room. In order to do so, you must put an ad in the local newspaper. You must use at least ten words in your ad, but no more than twenty-five words. Your telephone number counts as one of these words.

For Sale:

_____ _____ _____

_____ _____ _____

_____ _____ _____

_____ _____ _____

_____ _____ _____

_____ _____ _____

_____ _____ _____

_____

Said the Spider to the Fly

Pretend you are a spider. You want to invite Mr. Fly to your house for dinner. First, brainstorm some ideas that might convince him to come. Then write an invitation that includes the best of these ideas.

Dear Mr. Fly,

Response Activities

Response is not the same as evaluation; it is merely a quick reaction to the writing in general. A writer's strengths can be acknowledged and encouraged through this stage of the process, and good peer writing becomes a model for others in the class. Feedback through response helps clarify ideas and purposes, serves as a check for understanding, and can eliminate mechanical errors.

Teachers can provide response forms to help guide readers. The key to success with response sheets is to limit the amount of feedback. If you ask for too much information, the reader becomes confused and may respond poorly. As readers become familiar with the process of giving feedback, you can add and delete different response areas on the forms to help improve the paper or teach a specific skill. Here are a few ways to respond.

Partnerships

The easiest reader response occurs with partners. It is often less threatening for new writers to share their ideas with a partner than a larger group. The teacher can determine how pairs join. Use page 28 to encourage partner response.

Groups

As students progress in their writing skills, small groups may offer supportive and constructive response. For this activity, students share their papers in groups of four or five. Ask each group member to use the "P-Q-P" format of response.

P = *Praise* the part you like.
Q = Raise a *question* about an area that is unclear.
P = Make a suggestion to *polish* the paper.

A student reads his or her work to the group (or has it read), and the rest of the group members respond verbally or in writing. P-Q-P forms can be attached to first drafts, and used to help revise a final draft. A sample form can be found on page 29.

Parent or Other Adult

Parents respond to student work, by reading class sets or individual papers while using pre-established guidelines. One quick, easy, esteem-building way is to have the adults write two positive comments on each paper.

Total Class

Using reproduced copies, an overhead projector, or oral readings, the teacher directs the whole class response sessions, guiding students to go beyond vague likes and dislikes.

Exchange Program

Students' papers may be sent to another class within or outside of their own school for response. Establishing a relationship with a junior high or high school English class provides benefit to both groups. The elementary children are thrilled with the feedback from the older students and the secondary students hone their own writing skills in order to respond constructively.

Response

Partner Response

You are visiting your favorite place. You want to send a postcard to your best friend, describing this place for him or her. In your written description, "show" your friend why this place is so special.

Date _____

Dear _____ ,

_____

_____

_____

_____

_____

_____

_____

Your best friend,

_____

Reader's Name_____

1. Underline the parts you liked best in this writing.

2. Circle the part you want to know more about.

3. Write one sentence that tells why you would like to visit the place described in the postcard.

_____

_____

P-Q-P Response

_____   _____
         my name   *writer's name*

Praise:

I liked best the part about _____

_____

_____

_____

Question:

I did not understand _____

_____

_____

_____

Polish:

I think you could add something about _____

_____

_____

_____

Revision Activities

Revision means to add to a paper, not correct it. When students revise, they should not worry about grammatical errors except to clarify ideas. Using response sheets, such as the question from the P-Q-P method, helps students have a starting spot for revision.

Current research shows substantial evidence that the revision process itself is critical in improving writing. However, students would not take every piece of writing through a revision stage. Teachers should stress the careful development of a few choice assignments, rather than the hurried production of a great number of papers. Children find the revision process less painful when allowed to choose a favorite paper from several of their first drafts. It is important for them to understand that not all writing is worth revising, and that even the best writers feel this way.

Teachers must emphasize that the point of revision is to make the writing better, not to just change it for the sake of change. Practice with the class as a group by adding detail to paragraphs, changing the order of sentences to achieve sentence variety, and replacing overused, non-descriptive words with fresh, vivid ones. If possible, provide a first draft and a revised draft sample for students. Stress that there is not a right way or a wrong way to revise. Different authors approach each paper a different way.

Here are a few guidelines to help students revise.

- ◆ Require students to skip lines so they have room to add information.

- ◆ Encourage students to keep word banks so they have a collection of synonyms and adjectives to add to their writing.

- ◆ Remind students to start sentences with different words.

- ◆ Teach students to cut out each sentence in a sentence strip format, and try to put them together in a new order.

- ◆ Have students start small, and work up to larger, more complicated revisions.

- ◆ Tell students that they can revise a paper once, then put it away for a while. Later, they can reread their papers and revise again.

Graphic

The revision graphic on page 31 can be used as a coloring project to introduce the concept of revision, as a page in the students' individual writing folders, and/or as a focal point in your classroom writing center.

Editing & Rewriting Activities

Editing, the process of correcting mechanical errors, focuses students on the conventions of standard English, in areas such as spelling, punctuation, capitalization, and grammar. It is the last step before rewriting an assignment for publishing or other post-writing activities. Instruction in mechanics is most effective at this stage, especially in response to individual or whole class needs. Only papers going to the final draft stage should require editing.

Teachers should not become the sole editors of student papers. Instead, students should be taught the skills of editing. As with response sheet comments, introduce editing skills slowly. Do not expect students to look for and find all mechanical mistakes at once. Give students a list of editing symbols (page 33) and introduce one symbol at a time, slowly adding more as they demonstrate an understanding of the current area of study.

Start slowly with an example on the overhead projector or on a duplicated sheet that all students can see. Show students how to take one line at a time and read carefully. If they cover the lines below the one they are reading with a sheet of paper, it will increase their ability to focus on one area at a time.

Allow students to edit in pairs or small groups, using peer-editing worksheets. A sample is found on page 34. Attach this sheet to the paper that is to be edited, then distribute all papers for peer editing. Each student or group of students can correct for a specific type of error. For example, one group can become "capitalization specialists." You do not have to use all parts of the checklist. Ask your students to edit those areas in which they can experience editing success. As they become more proficient, add more areas of error for them to find.

If a child chooses to self edit, ask him or her to set the paper aside for a few days. Later, when the paper is reread, he or she will "see" it with a "fresh eye," and spot errors more easily. Use page 35 for editing and rewriting practice.

Here are some ideas to help with the editing process.

♦ Read your story aloud. Don't breathe until you come to an end punctuation mark. You might also make each end mark in the air.

♦ Find all the end punctuation marks and check to see that they are followed by capital letters.

♦ Search for all the proper names. Are they capitalized?

♦ Enlist the aid of others in your search. One person can correct for capitals, initial the paper, and pass it to person two. Person two corrects end punctuation, initals the paper, and passes it to person three who corrects spelling errors, and so forth.

When rewriting an edited paper for evaluation, attention should be given to form, neatness, and legibility, as well as adherence to the standards of written English. A rewritten paper should show a student's best effort.

Proofreading Marks

Editor's Mark	Meaning	Example
≡	Capitalize	<u>d</u>avid gobbled up the grapes.
/	Make lower case	My mother hugged Me when I came Home.
⊙	Add a period	The clouds danced in the sky⊙
Sp.	Spelling mistake	I laffed at the story.
∽	Reverse words or letters	How you are?
∧	Add a word	Would you pass the pizza?
⌄	Add a comma	I have two cats, two dogs and a goldfish.
ℓ	Delete (Get rid of)	Will you call call me on the phone tonight?

Peer Editing Worksheet

Writer's Name _____

Title of Paper _____

Editor(s) _____

_____

Read the student writing and fill out the parts of this list your teacher asks you to answer. Be sure to also make the corrections on the paper you are editing.

Questions	YES	NO
1. Do all sentences begin with a capital letter?		
2. Do all sentences end with the proper punctuation?		
3. Are all the words spelled correctly?		
4. Are all the names of people and places capitalized?		
5. Is the writing easy to read?		
6. Are there words missing?		
7. Are there extra words?		

Editing Practice

Correct the mistakes in the following paragraph. Use your "Proofreading Marks" sheet to help you.

My Whish

If i had a whish, i wood whish for a nu bik then i

cood ride ride it to skool then i wood lik a brite

Blue one with White handlbars. It wood realy fast

go. dad said i cood get a bik for my birthday.

Rewrite the edited paragraph, putting in the corrections you made.

_____

_____

_____

_____

_____

_____

_____

Skills Development Activities

During the editing phase of the writing process, lessons designed for skills development are logical and effective. In skills development, students learn and practice writing skills and mechanics. They can then transfer what they have learned to their editing jobs.

Many sources can be used for this stage, such as grammar books, teacher-created materials, and mechanics checklists. However, it is most effective if student papers serve as models for skill development lessons. For example, if your students consistently start their sentences with the same basic patterns, show them how to vary their sentence beginnings using a student paper and an overhead projector. Also show them examples of excellent student papers, pointing out the areas of well-done writing.

In the primary grades, skill development lessons need to be short and singly focused. If you give your students too many areas on which to concentrate, they may become frustrated and unable to apply what they have learned in self or peer editing situations. Follow each single-focus lesson with plenty of opportunities to master the skill being taught. After mastery, ask students to edit papers with the newly-acquired skill in mind.

Armed with a new skill and the ability to use it, your students will become confident proofreaders and an intregral part of the editing process!

◆ Task Cards

Practicing writing skills can be fun if you use task cards in the skills development area of your writing center. Sample task cards are found on page 38. Use them as they are or with adaptations to meet the needs of your students. Be sure to include task cards of your own design as well. Six blank task cards are provided for you on page 39.

◆ Sentence Lifting

Another way to focus on skills that need to be practiced is to "lift" sentences from the students' own work. This is especially effective if you see a problem that is common to many in the class. Simply find sentences in the students' work that will demonstrate the problem clearly. Write the sentences on the board or on an overhead transparency and have the class help correct them after a brief lesson from you about the proper mechanics.

◆ Daily Edit

Begin each morning with writing skills practice by placing a sentence or two on the board for the students to correct. Have them write the corrected sentence in the writing journal and add a note about why they made the correction that way. In addition to practicing looking for and correcting errors, the daily edit can be used to encourage more detailed writing. Post a very basic sentence and mark with a caret the places where additions could be made and underline "tired" words that could use substitutions.

The ∧ dog ∧ ran ∧. ➡ The huge black Doberman charged the masked intruder.

Graphic

The skills-development graphic on page 37 can be used as a coloring project to introduce skills development practice, as a page in the students' individual writing folders, and/or as a focal point in your class writing center.

Writing Skills Task Cards

TASK CARD: *Capitalization*

In the classroom on the wall under the clock, your teacher has posted a story with nine capitalization errors. Find them!

Rewrite the story with the corrections you have found.

TASK CARD: *Capitalization*

In the writing center you will find a cereal box. Rewrite a short part of something that is written on it, only as you write, make five capitalization errors.

Give your paper with errors to a friend to edit.

TASK CARD: *Capitalization*

Write a few sentences using the names of five people and places, but do not write these names with capitals.

Give your paper to a partner. See if he or she can be a successful capitalization detective!

TASK CARD: *Punctuation*

Read one or more of the pages from a book at this table. Recopy several of the sentences without end punctuation.

Give your paper with errors to a friend to edit.

TASK CARD: *Punctuation*

Read the paper posted on the wall by the door. Each time you see a comma, pause. Each time you see an end punctuation mark, take a breath.

Use this technique as you write your own papers or as you edit the papers of others.

TASK CARD: *Punctuation*

Make a list of contractions without putting apostrophes where they belong.

Give your paper to a partner. See if he or she can be a successful punctuation detective!

Task Cards

TASK CARD:

TASK CARD:

TASK CARD:

TASK CARD:

TASK CARD:

TASK CARD:

Evaluation Activities

When the rewrite has been completed to the author's satisfaction, it is ready to be evaluated. For many students, evaluation has meant only the grade that has been red-penned at the top of a paper. Teachers know, and need to keep in mind, that the purpose of evaluation is to promote growth. Feedback from evaluators should provide meaningful learning opportunities for writers, not just a grade.

For any evaluation to be a true measure of abilities, students must know who their evaluators will be and the criteria by which they will be judged. Vary the evaluators, using self, peer, teacher, parent, principal, librarian, community member, or children's magazine editor. Vary also the criteria by which they will be judged. Use holistic evaluations and student-generated rubrics. Choose specific areas to target on certain assignments, and evaluate only that area. For example, one assignment could be judged on creativity, another on mechanics, another on adherence to assignment guidelines. Most of all, be positive. Remember, writing is an ongoing process, and students who are encouraged will be most willing to keep trying.

Here are some general directions for creating a student-generated rubric for holistic grading. This can be used very well on a primary level if the names of the writers do not appear on the papers. Each student can be assigned a secret number, and these numbers can replace the names until "scoring" is done.

◆ Ask students to brainstorm the criteria of excellent papers. After they have a collection of ideas, let them choose four or five of the best ones. This will be a "5" paper. Continue this process for a good "4" paper, an average "3" paper, a poor "2" paper, and an unacceptable "1" paper. List the criteria for each level on a form such as the one on page 41. Students can keep a copy of the rubric in their own writing folders. You may also want to display it in your writing center.

◆ Before students evaluate each other, have them practice as a class with student-written (or teacher-written) examples. Be sure examples of all types of papers, excellent to unacceptable, are represented in the samples. Show students how to use the rubric as they read other students' papers, or have the papers read to them.

◆ Remember that looking for what makes a paper good reinforces those qualities in the writing that follows, and if the rubric has been student-generated, the goals are reachable.

Ideas for Creating a Rubric

"5" paper: imaginative ideas, advanced vocabulary, excellent printing or writing, mechanically correct, keeps reader's interest, many details

"4" paper: neat, understandable spelling, story can be followed, good punctuation, logical sequence, some detail

"3" paper: little if any description, quite a few spelling errors, punctuation errors, some parts difficult to read

"2" paper: poor mechanics and spelling, fragmented ideas, hard to read, listing of ideas rather than sentences of ideas

"1" paper: random words, no sentences, consistently incorrect or absent mechanics, difficult or impossible to read

"0" paper: no response, off-subject

Student Rubric

When you read someone's paper, give them a score based on the ideas listed below.

EXCELLENT PAPER "5"

_____

_____

_____

_____

_____

GOOD PAPER "4"

_____

_____

_____

_____

_____

OK PAPER "3"

_____

_____

_____

_____

_____

POOR PAPER "2"

_____

_____

_____

_____

UNACCEPTABLE PAPER "1"

_____

_____

_____

_____

Post-Writing/ Publishing Activities

The post-writing stage of the writing process refers to anything that happens to a piece of writing after it has been completed to an author's satisfaction. Post-writing gives students a chance to realize the value of their writing by sharing it with an audience. It is one of the most important steps in the writing process, for it showcases the students' ideas and hard work.

Post-writing can take on many forms. It can be as simple as posting student papers on classroom walls, or as involved as presenting a dramatization to the entire school. It can consist of reading a piece to a partner, or having a final draft published in a newspaper, magazine, or anthology. Sometimes the written draft will not be seen, but acted out with puppets or transformed into a skit to be videotaped and shown to a gathering of classmates, parents, and community members.

A sense of pride and a desire to improve one's writing is a natural extension of post-writing. The more you encourage your students to "publish" their work, the better their writing will become. Writers feel good about themselves and what they have accomplished when their work is read and valued by others. The post-writing graphic on page 43 can be used as a coloring project to introduce the concept of post-writing, as a page in the students' individual writing folders, and/or as a focal point in your class writing center.

Here are a few suggestions for post-writing activities.

1. Have exemplary writing read. Extend this oral presentation at a grade level or school assembly, parents' meeting, or community function.

2. Mail home a copy of the work.

3. Present to the principal or librarian the writing that has been determined to be the best writing of the week.

4. Create a "Writers' Showcase" for outstanding student writing.

5. Encourage students to enter writing contests.

6. Establish a community bulletin board to showcase writing.

7. Explore national and international markets for children's writing.

8. Exchange writing between classes and schools. You may wish to set up an intra-school or inter-district pen pal program. Exchange writing throughout the year and plan a get-together celebration at year's end.

9. Provide students with "practical" writing experiences, such as letters to the editor and requests for catalog products.

10. Assist students in preparing their writing for "publication" in another medium, such as audio or video tape.

11. Provide students with directions for making their own books. Examples of finished products should be on display in your writing center. One of these books could be a class book that has one piece of writing from each student. (See pages 44-53.)

Post-Writing and Publishing

Writers' Showcase

Publishing Center

Students need a place to be creative and to make their writing publishable. Some students will want to illustrate their work. Some will want to mount what they have done on colored paper. Others will want to add texture, magazine pictures, or cut-out lettering. A publishing center provides students this opportunity. If possible, try to set up this center in an area where supplies do not have to be put away and taken out again. Here is a list of possible supplies for your publishing center.

SUPPLIES

pens in a variety of colors	crayons
regular and colored pencils	paint
pencil sharpener	watercolors
markers in a variety of point sizes	tag board
calligraphy pens	stapler
construction paper	hole punch
lined and unlined paper	glue
old file folders	tape
wallpaper samples	scissors
contact paper	rulers
colored chalk	stencils
fixative	erasers
needles and thread	string
tissue paper	ribbon
old magazines and newspapers	stickers
greeting cards	old photographs
clip board	sponges
stamp pads and a variety of stamps	straws
fabric scraps	pressed plants
paint brushes in all sizes	wax paper
looseleaf rings	cellophane
scraps of yarn	food coloring
old shirts for smocks	work table
typewriter or word processor	paper towels
book binder and plastic spines	cleaning cloths
laminating supplies or access	paper cutter
water for clean up	parent volunteer

Publishing Center

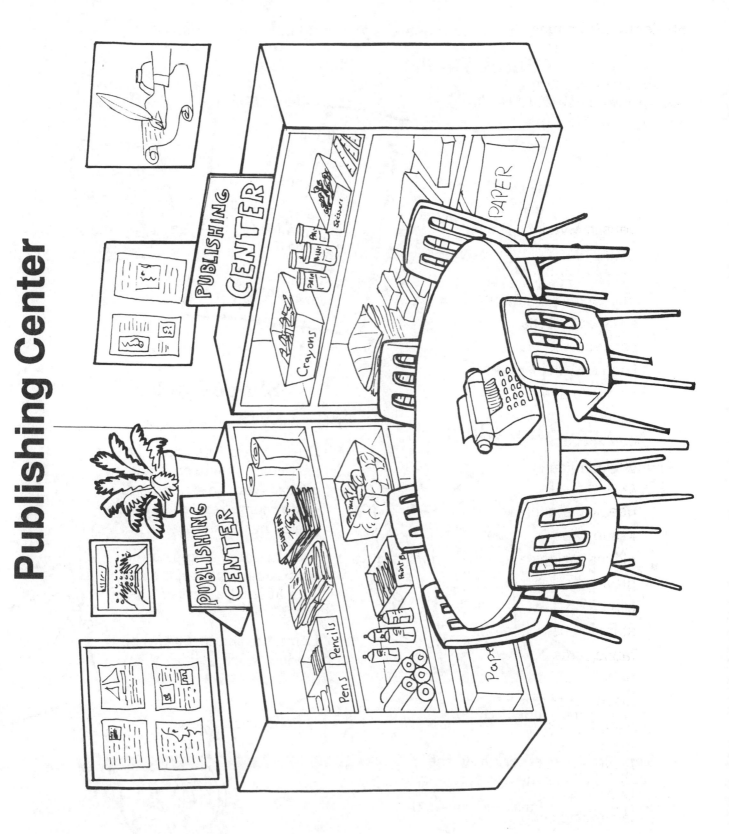

Types of Books

Here are a few of the many types of books your students can publish.

Plank Book

Here's a cover that won't rip!

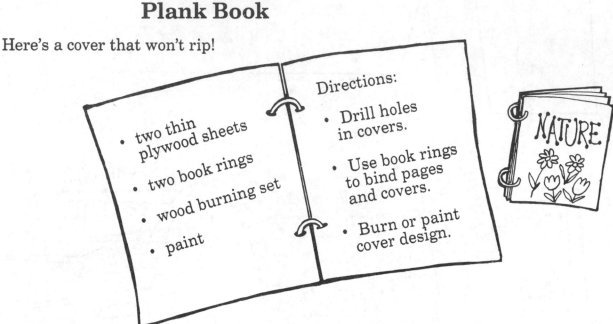

- two thin plywood sheets
- two book rings
- wood burning set
- paint

Directions:
- Drill holes in covers.
- Use book rings to bind pages and covers.
- Burn or paint cover design.

Accordion Book

How long can you go?

- Write and illustrate a story on paper strips. Each student could contribute a page.

- Tape strips together. Fold the sections of writing accordion-style.

- Staple or glue "heavier" covers to front and back for durability.

Shape Book

The variety is endless!

- Draw the outline of a particular theme on lined paper. Ask the students to write theme-related stories or poems in the shapes.

- Cut the same shape out of construction paper, making sure at least a part of it is on the fold.

- Laminate the cover and bind student work inside.

Types of Books *(cont.)*

Class Book

All About Nature

- Everyone writes and illustrates a page, including the teacher.
- Theme of book can be anything.

Favorite Sports

- Class can be divided into interest groups.
- Each group collaborates on a few pages to write about and illustrate, such as a soccer, swimming, baseball, and tennis section.

Group Book

Individual Book

I Remember When . . .

- Student writes and illustrates his or her own book.
- Another person could provide the illustrations for the author's text.

Pop-Up Books

Students of all ages enjoy creating these pop-up books!

1. Fold two pieces of 8½" x 11" (22 cm x 28 cm) paper in half from top to bottom. Set one piece aside.

2. Measure and mark 3 inches (8 cm) from each side along the fold. Cut a 2 inch (5 cm) slit at each mark.

3. Hold the paper so it looks like a tent. Push the cut portion all the way through and fold it down, creasing the inside fold.

4. Open the paper and see the amount of space on the pop-up area. Draw, color, and cut out the art that is to be popped up. Paste it to the area indicated.

5. Glue the second piece of paper as a cover on the first. By doing this, you won't see the hole that is left after the pop-up area has been cut out. Other pages can be added easily by gluing pages back to back. Individual pop-up pages can be put together for a class book!

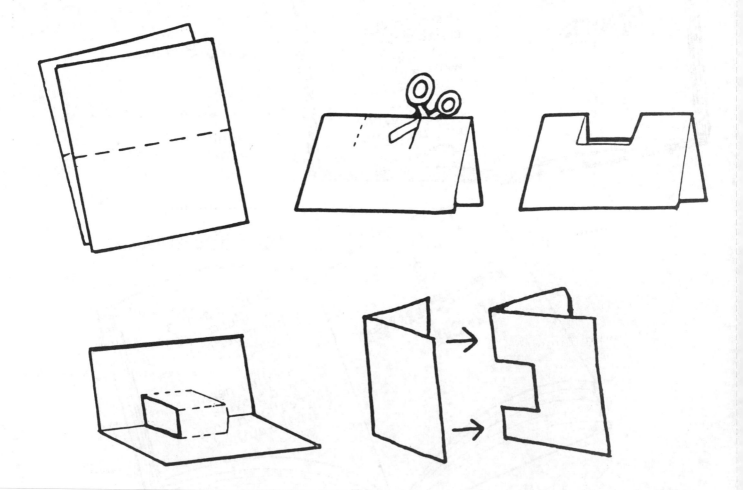

Pop-up Book Shapes

You can make pop-up books in shapes to support thematic teaching. Students can write theme-related stories and poems around the pop-up. When they have finished their writing, they can color and decorate the pop-up area and page with crayons, paints, construction paper, yarn, buttons, beads, and other appropriate art supplies.

Book Jackets

You can use book jackets for any assignment. They sit easily on a desk, and show off a student's work effectively. Book jackets are logical choices for book reports, too!

1. Select a color of 18" x 12" (45 cm x 30 cm) construction paper. Cut off 3 inches (7.5 cm) lengthwise, so paper is 18" x 9" inches (45 cm x 22.5 cm).

2. Measure 8 inches (20 cm) from one end and fold. Repeat with the other end. Paper will have two center folds when done.

3. Measure 3 inches (8 cm) from each end and fold. Your book jacket is ready to go!

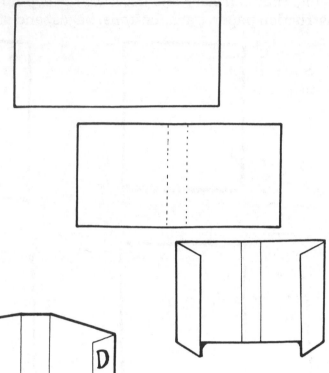

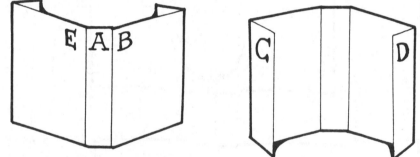

Write and/or illustrate the following in each area:

A. Title of book or assignment

   Student's name

B. Illustrated front cover with title repeated

C. A few made-up quotes about why this book or assignment should be read

   "Favorite book of all our second graders!"

   　　　— Lincoln Elementary

   "You won't be able to put it down!"

   　　　— Margie Davis

D. Information about the student author, such as an autobiographical sketch

E. Related assignment, such as a summary or a character profile for a book report; the written text of an original poem or story; or a re-written fairy tale

Book Making

Authors love to see their writing in real books!

1. Stack all the pages of the book in a neat pile.

2. Place a blank sheet of paper on the top and bottom of the pages.

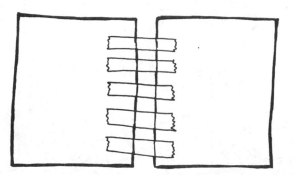

3. Leaving about a half-inch border, staple or sew all the pages together on the left side.

4. Place two pieces of light-weight cardboard side by side (cereal boxes work well.) Pieces should be ½" to 1" (1.3 cm to 2.54 cm) larger than the size of the pages in the book.

5. Leaving about 1" between them, tape the cardboard pieces together.

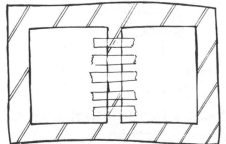

6. Put cardboard on top of the covering material, such as fabric, wallpaper, contact paper, or wrapping paper. Glue them together, leaving a 1" to 1½" (2.54 cm to 3.8 cm) material border.

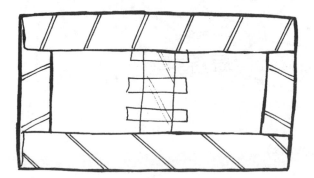

7. Fold up the edges of material over the cardboard and glue in place.

8. Glue the blank pages to the inside of the cardboard covers.

YOUR BOOK IS READY TO READ AND SHARE!

Publishing Addresses

Student writing can be sent to the following addresses. Check your professional journals for more sources.

Children's Playmate (ages 5-8)
c/o Children's Digest
1100 Waterway Blvd.
Indianapolis, Indiana 46206
(515) 280-3739
(800) 444-2704

Cricket (ages 6-12)
Cricket League
P.O. Box 593
Mount Morris, Illinois 61054-7666
(800) 827-0227

Highlights for Children (ages 2-11)
803 Church Street
Honesdale, Pennsylvania 18431

Stone Soup (ages 5-14)
P.O. Box 83
Santa Cruz, California 95063
(800) 447-4569

Jack and Jill
c/o Children's Digest
1100 Waterway Blvd.
Indianapolis, Indiana 46206
(515) 280-3739
(800) 444-2704

National Written and Illustrated by ...
(awards contest for students in all grade levels)
Write for rules and guidelines.
Landmark Editions, Inc.
P.O. Box 4469
Kansas City, Missouri 64127

Publishing Ideas

Have you ever . . .

worn it on a t-shirt? . . . asked to tack it to a community bulletin board? . . . phoned it to a grandparent? . . . served it on a platter? . . . sung it with a guitar? . . . framed it? . . . read it aloud? . . . had it published in a parents' newsletter? . . . written it in watercolor? . . . taped it as a radio program? . . . sent it to a local newspaper? . . . bound it in a book? . . . hung it in your room? . . . performed it for an assembly? . . . written it in fresh snow? . . . read it in a poetry parade? . . . sent it to a nursing home? . . . read it over the school's public address system? . . . written it in a cookbook? . . . drawn it on a graffiti mural with permission? . . . sent it to a sick classmate? . . . written it to a pen pal? . . . told it to a pet? . . . presented it in an animated film or comic strip? . . . written it in chalk on your driveway? . . . made a poster of it? . . . entered it in a contest? . . . flown it across the room on a paper airplane? . . . stitched it on fabric? . . . written it on an original calendar you have tried to sell? . . . performed it in a puppet show? . . . bound it and placed it in the library? . . . sent it in a letter to a published author? . . . made it a message in a bottle? . . . written it in sand? . . . sent it to a political figure such as your mayor, congress representative, or the President? . . . performed it as a skit in a shopping mall? . . . submitted it to a magazine? . . . read it to a school employee such as the principal's secretary or a cafeteria worker? . . . Magic-Markered it on a sheet? . . . mailed it to a former teacher? . . . saved it in a time capsule for the future? . . . sent it in a class mailbox? . . . illustrated it for a Valentine? . . . read it to the class? . . . tucked it away to be read and enjoyed when you are older?

Writing Across the Curriculum

Writing is not just for writing time. Every curricular area presented to a child can provide an opportunity for teaching and reinforcing writing skills. Many times a simple teacher direction such as those on this page will inspire written expression that increases understanding of the subject as well as providing practice for developing writing skills.

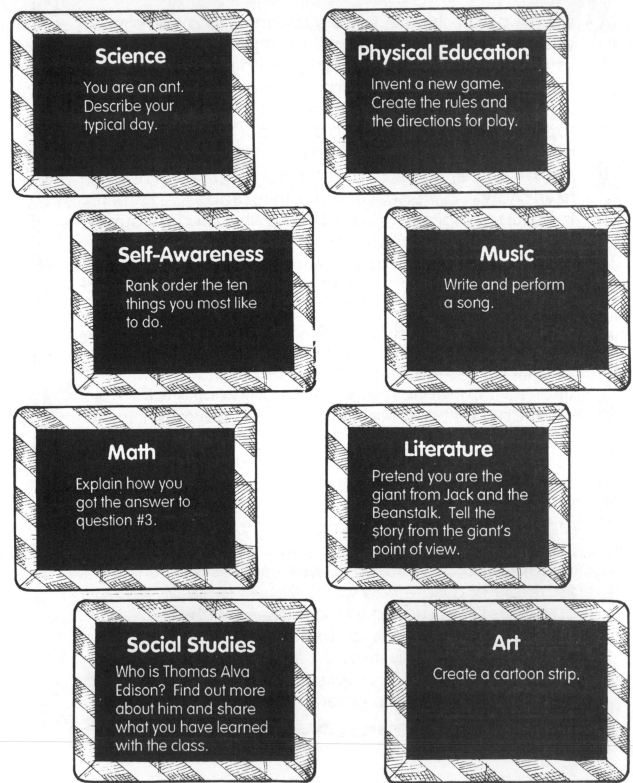

Science
You are an ant. Describe your typical day.

Physical Education
Invent a new game. Create the rules and the directions for play.

Self-Awareness
Rank order the ten things you most like to do.

Music
Write and perform a song.

Math
Explain how you got the answer to question #3.

Literature
Pretend you are the giant from Jack and the Beanstalk. Tell the story from the giant's point of view.

Social Studies
Who is Thomas Alva Edison? Find out more about him and share what you have learned with the class.

Art
Create a cartoon strip.

54

Ideas

Literature

- Read *The Whingdingdilly* by Bill Peet or *Oliphaunt* by J.R.R. Tolkien. Encourage the children to draw the animal they hear described as the story or poem is read. After reading, share the pictures. Then ask your students to complete the activity on page 57.

- To focus on character analysis, have students create a "Wanted Poster" for a character from a story they have read. Have them draw a picture of this wanted character in the box in the center of the poster on page 58. Then have them complete it by writing appropriately on the lines below the picture.

- If you are looking for a primary book to model letter writing, share *The Jolly Postman or Other People's Letters* by Janet and Allan Ahlberg. Page 59 provides a sample letter-writing activity.

- After reading *There's a Nightmare in My Closet* by Mercer Mayer, ask your students to think about a time a monster they imagined scared them. Brainstorm things they remember about their creatures, such as physical description, places they thought it was hiding, what it could do to them, and how they handled their fear. After the brainstorming session, ask for volunteers to complete the assignment on page 60 and share their finished papers with the class. Those students without "monster experience" can create a fictional monster.

- After a thematic unit on bears, which included but was not limited to reading bear stories, learning about their habits and habitats, researching the history of specific bear types, singing bear songs, cooking bear-shaped cookies, and making related art projects, ask your students to create a bear shape story. It could be a continuation of a story they have heard or read, or an original story based on bear knowledge they have gathered during your unit. Use as many of the shapes on page 61 as is necessary for story completion. Trace the outline on colored paper for a cover and staple it into a book.

- See page 62 for complete directions for creating story boards and their follow-up activities based on favorite fairy tales.

Science

- Read *A Drop of Blood* by Paul Showers to your class. Encourage them to visualize what you read. Stop and try some of the activities or ideas mentioned in the book, such as using a flashlight to see their own blood, drawing a white cell trapping germs, or calculating the amount of blood in the bodies of people of different sizes. Discuss the scientific concepts mentioned in the book. For a creative writing activity, ask your students to imagine that they are a single drop of blood. Invite them to tell a story or a poem from the blood's point of view! Page 63 provides a form for this activity.

- Use any or all of the activity cards on page 64 during a unit on weather.

Math

- Connecting writing and math is not as difficult as it may seem. See page 65 for several examples.

- Read *Moira's Birthday* by Robert Munsch. Discuss estimation skills and realistic planning! Then have your students work in groups to use page 66 to plan a BIG party.

Ideas *(cont.)*

Social Studies

- Creating games and puzzles are wonderful writing activities to help develop social studies vocabulary. Directions for creating a Word Search may be found on page 67.

- Another way to relate writing to social studies is described in detail on page 68, "An Ink Blot in History."

Art

- Writing about a piece of artwork they have created will stretch students' imaginations. Use page 69 to practice writing about art. Then have students write about other works they create.

- By following the directions on page 70 you will be able to direct your students to create a "Me-Mobile" that combines writing and art.

Music

- Read farm animal books such as *The Very Busy Spider* by Eric Carle, *Wake Up, Sun!* by David L. Harrison, *Our Animal Friends At Maple Hill Farm* by Alice and Martin Provensen, and *The Midnight Farm* by Reeve Lindbergh. Follow your reading with farm songs such as "Grandpa's Farm," "The Farmer in the Dell," and "Old MacDonald Had a Farm." Ask your students to choose farm animals from your reading and singing. Have them write songs about these animals and sing them to friends or your entire class.

- For a list of children's literature books that relate to music, see page 71. Use books such as these to model and stimulate writing about music.

Physical Education

- Direct students to write a plan for teaching the class to play a game or sport. Have them use page 72. Then let those who wish to do so conduct a physical education class using their plan.

- Students often have strong positive or negative feelings about physical education activities. Use the shapes on pages 73 to 75 to help them write about their feelings.

Self-Awareness

- Read *Guess Who My Favorite Person Is* by Byrd Baylor. Play the "tell-what-your-favorite-thing-is" game. You must play it according to the rules set forth in the book. Here is an example. What is your favorite color? A wrong answer would be "blue." The answer is wrong because the person who answered did not say what kind of blue was the favorite. A correct answer would be "the kind of blue on a lizard's belly." This answer is correct because detail gave us the shade of favorite blue. Follow this oral activity with the writing assignment on page 75. This is a great activity for increasing detail in writing!

- Helping children develop a positive self-image is paramount in the primary years. There is a wealth of books that can help you build a child's self-esteem, and many writing activities that can be generated from these books. A few of these can be found on page 77.

I Imagine. . .

Choose an animal, real or imagined, to describe for your classmates. Draw a picture of the animal you have chosen. Write a vivid description of this animal in story or poetic form. Read your writing to the class and ask them to draw the animal they see as they hear your words. Then, share your picture with your classmates. How do your animals compare?

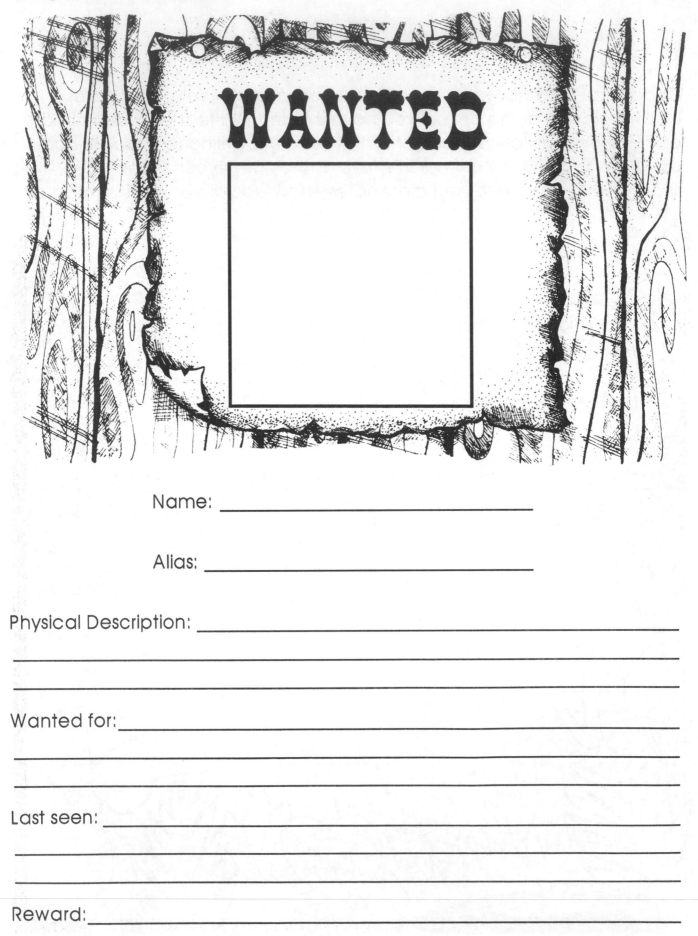

Name: _____

Alias: _____

Physical Description: _____
_____
_____

Wanted for: _____
_____
_____

Last seen: _____
_____
_____

Reward: _____

Letter from Camp

Imagine you have just met one of the characters in your story at a summer camp. You know you are going to become good friends! Write a letter to your parents telling them about your new friend. Be sure to describe his or her physical appearance, reveal something about his or her personality, and relate some camp experience to an event that happened in the story.

Dear _____ ,

Love,

My Monster

1. Where is your monster hiding? _____

2. What does your monster look like?

   _____

   _____

3. What does your monster like to do?

   _____

   _____

4. Is your monster afraid of something? If so, what does it fear?

   _____

5. How did you or would you deal with your monster?

   _____

   _____

Draw your monster here.

Bear Shape Stories

Fairy Tale Story Boards

Brainstorm a list of fairy tales.

Write all titles on the board.

Ask a student or a group of students to retell the story of *The Three Little Pigs*. Encourage the class to imagine how the story would have been different had it been told from the wolf's point of view. Invite them to share their new point of view story ideas with the class.

Read *The True Story of the 3 Little Pigs* by Jon Scieszka. Ask the class what they liked or did not like about this retelling of a familiar tale.

Divide students into small groups and ask them to choose a fairy tale with which they all are familiar. All group members must agree on the same story, and it should not be a story another group has chosen.

Ask each group to draw pictures of at least eight significant scenes from the story. Two large sheets of construction paper, each folded into four sections and taped together work well. They are creating a story board for the fairy tale that is similar to the creation of frames for a comic strip.

For example:

Each student group will create and perform a play based on some or all of the scenes they have chosen for their story board. It will be their own version of the story, perhaps utilizing a different point of view as was done telling *The True Story of the 3 Little Pigs*. Tell them that parts of the story may be left out and original parts added. Remind them that it is their version! Each group member must have a speaking part. Encourage the use of a narrator, costumes or paper bag puppets, scenery, sound effects, and dramatic presentation.

A Drop of Blood

Hi, I am a drop

of _____'s blood.

child's name

_____

_____

_____

_____

_____

_____

_____

_____

_____

Weather Writing Activities

Use any or all of these activity cards during your unit on weather.

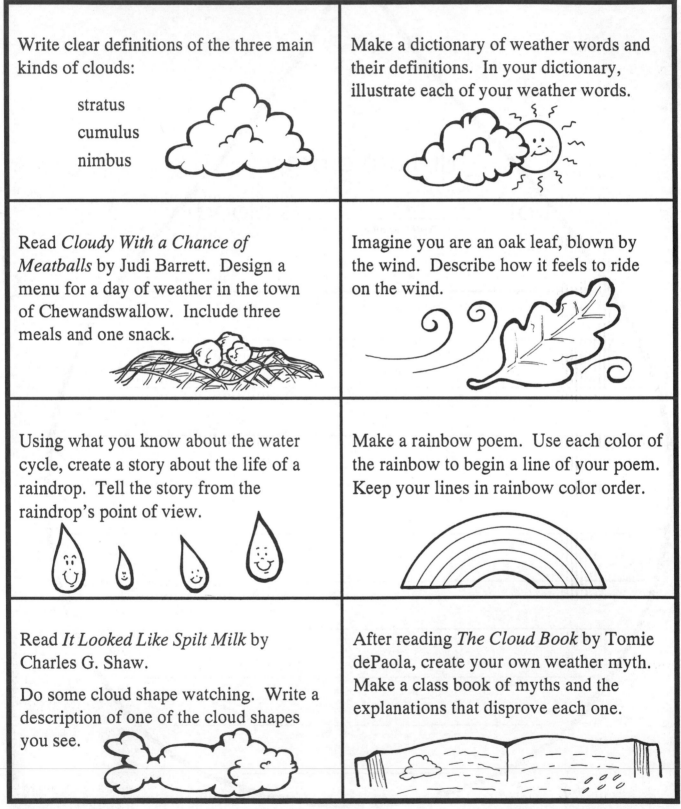

Write clear definitions of the three main kinds of clouds:

stratus

cumulus

nimbus

Make a dictionary of weather words and their definitions. In your dictionary, illustrate each of your weather words.

Read *Cloudy With a Chance of Meatballs* by Judi Barrett. Design a menu for a day of weather in the town of Chewandswallow. Include three meals and one snack.

Imagine you are an oak leaf, blown by the wind. Describe how it feels to ride on the wind.

Using what you know about the water cycle, create a story about the life of a raindrop. Tell the story from the raindrop's point of view.

Make a rainbow poem. Use each color of the rainbow to begin a line of your poem. Keep your lines in rainbow color order.

Read *It Looked Like Spilt Milk* by Charles G. Shaw.

Do some cloud shape watching. Write a description of one of the cloud shapes you see.

After reading *The Cloud Book* by Tomie dePaola, create your own weather myth. Make a class book of myths and the explanations that disprove each one.

Writing About Math

Create a chart that shows sorting and classification skills based on literature that you have read, such as *Frog and Toad Are Friends* by Arnold Lobel and *Harriet's Halloween Candy* by Nancy Carlson. In writing, explain the sorting methods you used.

Make word problems for three of the math problems you solved today.

If Amy had 10 paper clips in her pocket on her way to school and lost four of them, how many would she have?

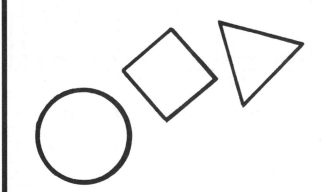

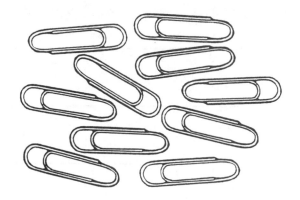

Create a story using geometrical shapes such as circles, squares, rectangles, and triangles.

Read *The Secret Birthday Message* by Eric Carle and *Grandfather Tang's Story* by Ann Tompert for ideas.

You have been given ten dollars to spend in any way you wish.

Make a list of what you would buy and how much each item costs. Write an explanation of why you chose each of the items you did!

Read *Alexander, Who Used to Be Rich Last Sunday* by Judith Viorst for a pre or post activity.

What a Party!

Work with a partner or in a small group to plan the menu for a party with 200 children as your guests. Calculate the expense of the menu as well.

Item	Cost Per Item	Number Needed	Total Cost

Write the dialogue that you would have with your parents if you asked them for a party with the menu you have planned above.

_____

_____

_____

_____

_____

_____

Word Search Puzzle

1. Choose ten people, places, events, and/or things from the social studies area you are studying. Write one word by each number.

   1. _____   6. _____

   2. _____   7. _____

   3. _____   8. _____

   4. _____   9. _____

   5. _____   10. _____

2. Write your words, one letter at a time, in the squares on the grid below. You may write your words across or down. Spread your words around to different areas on the grid.

3. Fill in the remaining squares with other letters of the alphabet. Vary the arrangement of the letters.

4. Switch papers with a classmate. Can all the words be found and circled?

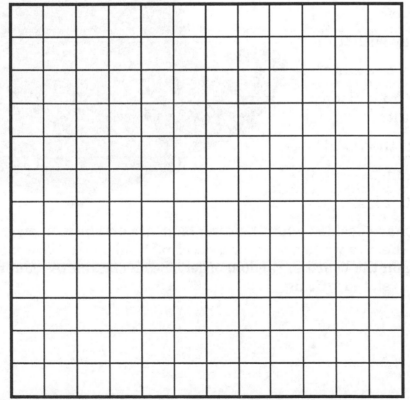

An Ink Blot in History

1. Choose a social studies topic you have already taught, and ask students to brainstorm everything that comes to mind on this topic. Record all ideas on board or overhead.

2. Read *It Looked Like Spilt Milk* by Charles G. Shaw to the class. Before you read the words on each page, let the class determine what the "milk blot" might be.

3. Give each student a large piece of white drawing paper. Put a large, randomly-shaped drop of black paint in the middle of each paper. Instruct students to fold their papers in half to smear the paint.

4. Guide them in slowly opening the folded paper and ask them to study their blots. Remind them of the social studies word and ideas list that is on the board. Invite the students to imagine their blot is something from the list, or related to the topic in some way. Tell them there are no right or wrong answers.

5. Ask students questions about the "social studies" ink blot on their papers.

    *   Is this a souvenir from another time in history?

    *   Does it have a name?

    *   Where did it come from?

    *   Does someone need it?

    *   Is it alive?

    *   Did it change history?

    *   In what historical time was it most popular?

    *   Could you play with it?

    *   Is it a country or a state?

    *   Did someone from history wear it or eat it?

    *   Can it change the world?

    *   Do you want one?

    *   How long will it last?

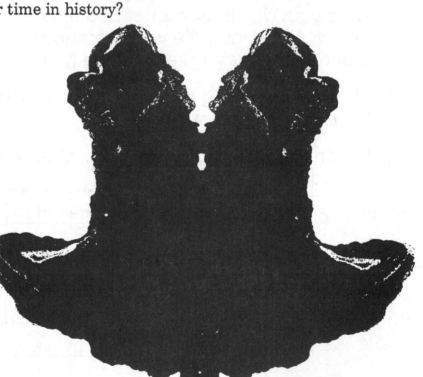

6. After students have decided what their ink blots are and have answered several questions, ask them to write a story or a description about it. Post ink blots and the related writing on the board in random order. See if classmates can match the ink blots with their related writing.

What Is It?

Use your imagination to finish the picture below. Turn your paper any way you wish to help you think of ideas. When your picture is finished, write two sentences about what you have created.

Write one sentence to explain your drawing.

_____

_____

_____

Write one sentence to explain something your drawing does.

_____

_____

_____

A Me-Mobile

On different colored construction paper, help students outline their hands and their bare feet and carefully cut out their tracings.

On each finger, students will write their answers to "me" questions. On the middle section of each hand, ask them to draw something that is important to them.

Sample "Me" questions for fingers:

I am _____ years old.

I am good at _____ .

I seem to be _____ .

My birthday is _____ .

I have _____ hair and _____ eyes.

I am _____ .

I am not _____ .

I like to _____ .

I don't like to _____ .

I have never _____ .

A word that describes me is _____ .

Add some more questions of your own!

On each toe, students will write one of their "favorites." On one of the large foot sections, ask them to draw a picture of a place they have been to or would like to go. On the other large section, ask them to draw a picture of their favorite outdoor activity.

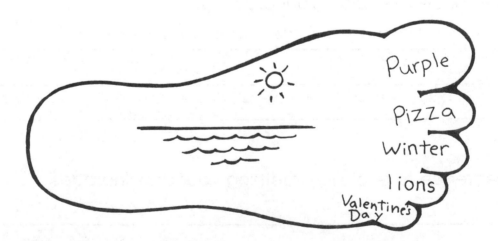

Hang both hands and feet from a hanger to make a "Me-Mobile!"

Music in Children's Literature

Here is a partial listing of current literature that involves music in some way.

Books that contain musical scores or lyrics:

Abiyoyo by Pete Seeger (Macmillan, 1986)

All the Pretty Horses by Susan Jeffers (Scholastic, 1974)

The Drinking Gourd by F.N. Munjo (Harper & Row, 1983)

Frog Went A-Courtin' by John Langstaff (HBJ, 1955)

Four & Twenty Dinosaurs by Bernard Most (Harper & Row, 1990)

Hush Little Baby by Jeanette Winter (Pantheon, 1984)

in a cabin in a wood adapted by Darcie McNally (Cobblehill, 1991)

Lizard's Song by George Shannon (Greenwillow, 1981)

Mama Don't Allow by Thacher Hurd (Harper & Row, 1984)

Mary Had A Little Lamb by Mary Josepha Hale (Holiday, 1984)

Mary Wore Her Red Dress and Henry Wore His Green Sneakers adapted and illustrated by Merle Peek (Clarion, 1985)

Oh, A-Hunting We Will Go by John Langstaff (McElderry, 1974)

The Pea Patch Jig by Thacher Hurd (Crown, 1986)

Really Rosie by Maurice Sendak (Harper & Row, 1975)

Song of the Swallows by Leo Politi (Aladdin, 1949)

There Was An Old Lady Who Swallowed A Fly illustrated by Pam Adams (Child's Play, 1989)

Books in which a character sings or plays an instrument:

Bedtime for Frances by Russell Hoban (Harper & Row, 1960)

The Foolish Frog by Pete and Charles Seeger (Macmillan, 1973)

Love You Forever by Robert Munsch (Firefly, 1988)

Song and Dance Man by Karen Ackerman (Knopf, 1988)

Strega Nona by Tomie dePaola (Prentice-Hall, 1975)

Books that refer to musical instruments or musical compositions:

Amy the Dancing Bear by Carly Simon (Doubleday, 1989)

Apt. 3 by Ezra Jack Keats (Aladdin, 1986)

Drummer Hoff by Barbara Emberley (Simon & Schuster, 1967)

CRASH! BANG! BOOM! by Peter Spier (Doubleday, 1972)

I Like the Music by Leah Komaiko (Harper & Row, 1987)

Peter and the Wolf by Sergei Prokofiev (Knopf, 1986)

When Clay Sings by Byrd Baylor (Aladdin, 1972)

Books about music for children:

Eyewitness Books: Music by Neil Ardley (Knopf, 1989)

The Oxford First Companion to Music by Kenneth and Valerie McLeish (Oxford University Press, 1982)

The Philharmonic Gets Dressed by Karla Kuskin (Harper & Row, 1982)

My P.E. Lesson Plan

Pretend you are a teacher and you are going to teach a class how to play a game or sport you enjoy. Prepare your lesson on this planning sheet.

Equipment:

What equipment do you need to play?

_____

_____

_____

Description:

How do you play?

_____

_____

_____

Rules:

What are the rules necessary for playing?

_____

_____

_____

Evaluation:

Why do you like to play this game or sport?

_____

_____

_____

Physical Education

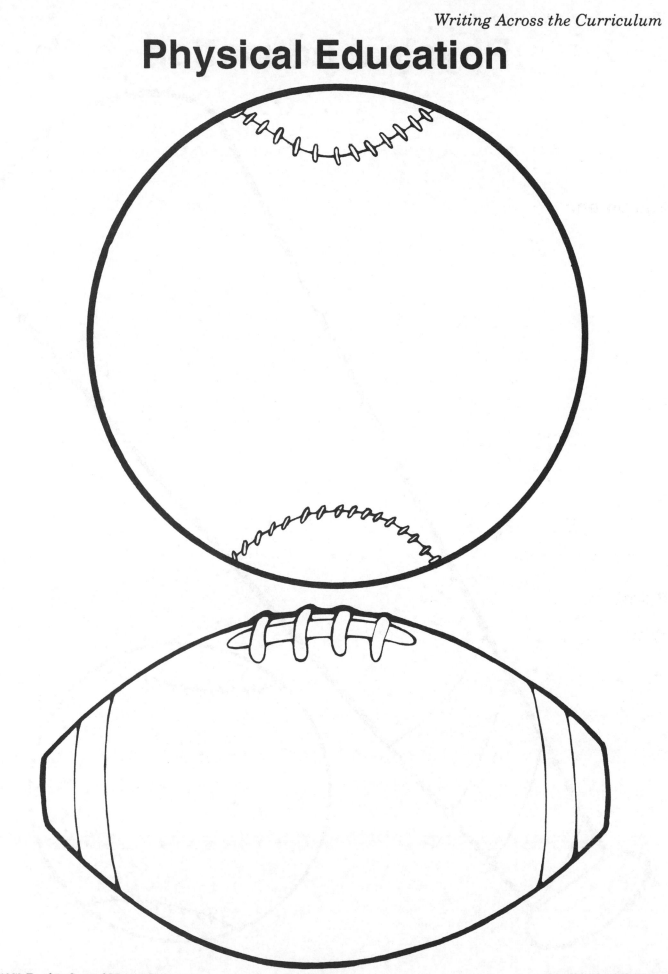

Physical Education

Physical Education

My Favorites

Use many details to describe your favorites.

Favorite color:_____

_____

Favorite thing to touch:_____

_____

Favorite sound:_____

_____

Favorite place to live: _____

_____

Favorite dream: _____

_____

Favorite thing to see moving: _____

_____

Favorite thing to taste:_____

_____

Favorite smell:_____

_____

Favorite time of day: _____

_____

76

Esteem-Building Activities

◆ Read *I Wish I Were a Butterfly* by James Howe.

Self-esteem concept: Just because someone says something bad about you doesn't mean you have to believe it. You, and people who really care about you, know what the truth is.

Activity: Each class member makes a butterfly shape using the art materials you have available. Working in groups of three or four, group members each write one positive comment on the butterflies of other group members. Display the completed butterflies in the class.

◆ Read *Arthur's Eyes* and *Arthur's Nose* by Marc Brown.

Self-esteem concept: Fix the things you can change about yourself and accept the things you cannot. Everyone has something about them that makes them different. It is fine to be different. Accept who you are and others will, too.

Activity: Use an inking pad to make a fingerprint on the top of a white piece of paper. Each fingerprint is different just as each child is different. Under the fingerprint, write two or more things about you that make you different from others. Explain why you like your differences.

◆ Read *Leo the Late Bloomer* by Robert Kraus.

Self-esteem concept: Everyone develops at a different rate. Sometimes it takes time, but you'll get there!

Activity: Make a hand-held mirror shape out of tag or other lightweight cardboard. Attach a piece of aluminum foil to the "mirror" part. Think of two or more things you do well. Using a blunt point of a pencil, etch these things on the mirror you have made. Be proud of what you can do!

EXCELLENCE

In honor of

in writing

I present this certificate of achievement

to

_____
name

on this _____ day of _____ , _____
date   month   year

_____
teacher's signature

78

To the teacher: Duplicate this page on goldenrod paper.

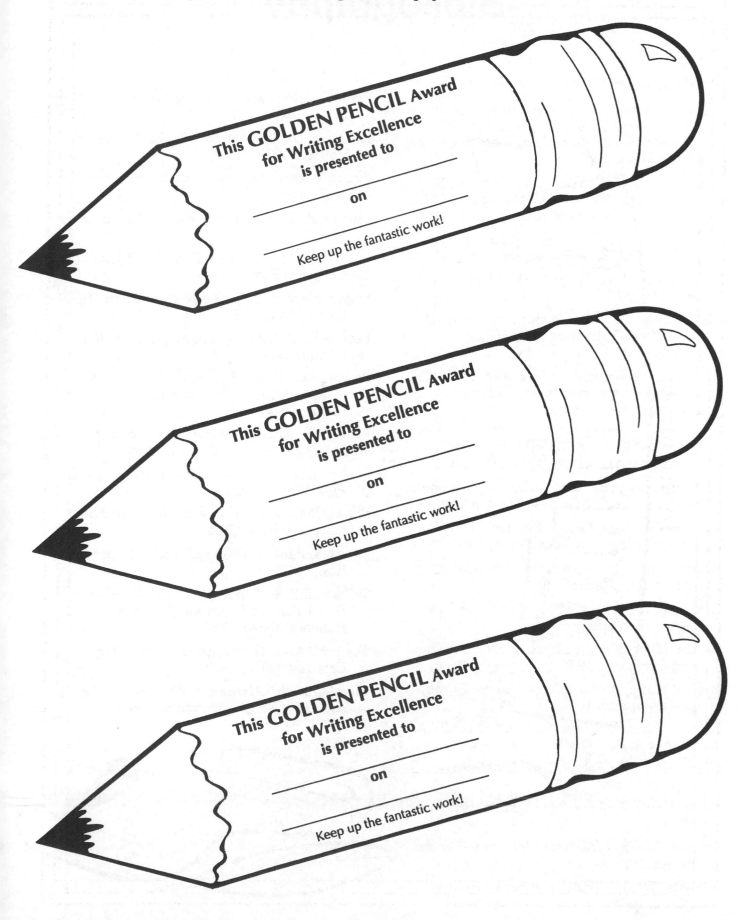

This **GOLDEN PENCIL** Award
for **Writing Excellence**
is presented to
_____
on
_____
Keep up the fantastic work!

This **GOLDEN PENCIL** Award
for **Writing Excellence**
is presented to
_____
on
_____
Keep up the fantastic work!

This **GOLDEN PENCIL** Award
for **Writing Excellence**
is presented to
_____
on
_____
Keep up the fantastic work!

Bibliography

Professional Resources

Daniels, Harvey and Steven Zemelman. *A Writing Project: Training Teachers of Composition From Kindergarten to College*. Heinemann, 1985.

Frank, Marjorie. *If You're Trying to Teach Kids How to Write, You've Gotta Have This Book*. Inventive Publications, 1979

Graves, Donald H. *Writing: Teachers & Children At Work*. Heinemann, 1983

Irvine, Joan. *How To Make POP-UPs*. Morrow, 1987

Parry, Jo-Ann and David Hornsby. *Write On: A Conference Approach To Writing*. Heinemann, 1985

Vitale, Barbara Meister. *Unicorns Are Real — A Right Brain Approach to Learning*. Jalmar Press, 1988

Literature Selections Recommended In This Book

Ahlberg, Janet and Allan. *The Jolly Postman or Other People's Letters*. Heinemann, 1986

Arvetis, Chris and Carole Palmer. *What Is a Cloud?* Weekly Reader Books, 1986

Barrett, Judi. *Cloudy with a Chance of Meatballs*. Aladdin, 1982

Baylor, Byrd. *Guess Who My Favorite Person Is*. Aladdin, 1985

Brown, Marc. *Arthur's Eyes*. Little, Brown and Company, 1979

Brown, Marc. *Arthur's Nose*. Little, Brown and Company, 1976

Brown, Margaret Wise. *The Important Book*. Harper & Row, 1949

Carle, Eric. *The Secret Birthday Message*. Harper & Row, 1986

Carle, Eric. *The Very Busy Spider*. Scholastic, 1984

Carlson, Nancy. *Harriet's Halloween Candy*. Puffin, 1984

dePaola, Tomie. *The Cloud Book*. Holiday House, 1975

Freeman, Don. *A Rainbow of My Own*. Viking Press, 1978

Harrison, David L. *Wake Up, Sun!* Random House, 1986

Kraus, Robert. *Leo the Late Bloomer*. Simon and Schuster, 1971

Lindbergh, Reeve. *The Midnight Farm*. Dial, 1987

Lobel, Arnold. *Frog and Toad Are Friends*. Harper & Row, 1979

Mayer, Mercer. *There's a Nightmare in My Closet*. Dial, 1968

Peet, Bill. *The Whingdingdilly*. Houghton Mifflin, 1976

Provensen, Alice and Martin. *Our Animal Friends at Maple Hill Farm*. Random House, 1974

Provensen, Alice and Martin. *The Year at Maple Hill Farm*. Aladdin, 1988

Scieszka, John. *The True Story of the 3 Little Pigs*. Viking, 1989

Shaw, Charles G. *It Looked Like Spilt Milk*. Harper & Row, 1988

Showers, Paul. *A Drop of Blood*. Harper & Row, 1989

Tolkien, J.R.R. "Oliphaunt" *The Random House Book of Poetry for Children*. Random House, 1983

Tompert, Ann. *Grandfather Tang's Story*. Crown, 1990

Viorst, Judith. *Alexander, Who Used to Be Rich Last Sunday*. Aladdin, 1988